HOW TO TELL A TORNADO

HOW TO TELL
A TORNADO

HOWARD MOHR

A Prairie Home Companion Book

Howard Mohr is heard regularly on live broadcasts of "A Prairie Home Companion" over public radio stations across the country. He lives near Cottonwood in southwestern Minnesota with his wife and daughter.

Some of the poems and stories have appeared in *The Co-op Country News, The Worthington Daily Globe, Minnesota Products, Survivor's Manual, Charas, Minnesota English Journal, Dacotah Territory, Poets of South-western Minnesota, Three Rivers Poetry Journal,* and *Zero Makes Me Hungry* (Scott, Foresman).

"A Minnesota Farmers Speaks," "Widow Before the Auction," and "The Dying Race" copyright Rodale Press.

Design by Susan Baleiko

ISBN 0-942110-02-1

CONTENTS

HOW TO TELL A TORNADO

HOW TO TELL A TORNADO

Listen for noises.
If you do not live
near railroad tracks,
the freight train you hear
is not the Northern Pacific
lost in the storm:
that is a tornado
doing imitations of itself.
One of its favorite sounds
is no sound.
After the high wind, and
before the freight train,
there is a pocket
of nothing:
this is when you think
everything has stopped:
but do not be fooled.
Leave it all behind
except for a candle
and take to the cellar.

Afterwards
if straws are imbedded
in trees without leaves,
and your house — except
for the unbroken bathroom mirror —
has vanished
without a trace,
and you are naked
except for the right leg
of your pants,
you can safely assume
that a tornado
has gone through your life
without touching it.

CAT SAILING

I love the county roads at night
when the moon is full, just as spring
starts pushing this and that thing
up and up, and everything living
wants to love a little and live
a little more: you know what I mean,
but for the record, that includes
apple trees, box elder bugs, hogs,
green worms, bluegrass, skunks,
and, oh yes, people. It's a good time
to sell life insurance and protection
for the stuff you collect inside.
But it's night that's best,
alone in a car that propels itself
by exploding trees and dinosaurs
a million years old.
And here and there, you find a squashed cat,
a tom on his way to that farm by smell,
a female in heat, surprised once and for all,
but both dead as a Frisbee
and inorganic as a college degree.
You stop by the side of the road
and take that mortar board feline
by its side and sail it into the small grain
crops just coming up. You are thrilled
the way its smooth fur catches
the light of the moon, the stillness
when it lands, the exhilaration
you feel having made something dead
pass through the air
like an unidentified flying object.
Back in the car, back down the road.
Going home to wait for summer,
and fall, and winter again, then spring,
then summer, then fall, then winter.
That's the way it goes,
one after the other.
It's a lovely system, invented by
somebody with a sense of rhythm
and no eye for detail.

2

Waving in the rural midwest on the face of it seems like a simple, direct way of saying hello from a distance. The key word is *seems*, because although I have been waving for many years now, I still get caught in situations where I think a wave is called for, but am not sure how to wave or when to wave. So you can imagine what happens to a newcomer in the country.

First of all, waving from a vehicle to another person in a vehicle or on the ground (whether at home or in the field), is a rural act. People wave in the city, it's true, but it just doesn't mean as much, and besides that, it's a different kind of wave. I never feel right waving in the city. And while I'm on the subject, let me say that getting another person on a CB is not equivalent to a wave. You hear people talk like it is, but it's not, and never will be.

Basically most waves occur when one or both persons are in vehicles. No waving situation develops when both people are out of their vehicles, because a wave definitely involves the *passing process*, where one or both are *going by*. Most of the waving situations involve two vehicles traveling in the opposite direction meeting and passing. But let me talk about a few unusual forms of waving first.

If you are on the ground — sawing down elm trees, walking beans, changing the oil on the tractor — and a vehicle goes by on the road, the whole responsibility for starting the wave process is yours: you look up or don't look up. If you look up, then you will wave if you know the person and they know you. You may wave if you don't know the person, *if the other person waves first*. On rare occasions, you may wave first at a perfect stranger going by in a Winnebago or a '64 Chrysler if they look like they need a wave. This is the "good will" wave, and is not to be discounted.

If you are filling the corn planter at the end of the rows, holding the sack with both hands, you do not look up or let go of the seed bag, in order to wave. If you do look up, the most you should do is give a short backward flip of the head. If you are in the car, simply reverse the above directions. We might as well stress here that honking is mostly forbidden and will get you into trouble or make people think you are a stranger, unless the other person just got married, has a new tractor or pickup, or you notice oats leaking from the truck where the rags fell out. In any case a short toot is enough.

Never wave more than once if the same situation develops again in the same day. That is, if you drive by again and the person on the ground is engaged in the same activity, do not wave. He will probably not look up. But if he is doing something different, the wave is optional. You wave twice at a person only if on the second time by they have either changed vehicles (bigger tractor, tractor to truck), or changed grains (hauling corn first time, beans second). If they have only changed clothes or hats, you should not wave again, usually.

Now the rest of my remarks can be applied to all situations, but are particularly aimed at the vehicle to vehicle wave, as for instance, tractor to tractor, combine to swather, or — a not uncommon thing — motorcycle to tractor. Winter waving is the same as summer waving, except that snowmobiling is in a category by itself.

SIGHTING: Begin evaluating the vehicle approaching as far ahead as possible. Is it my neighbor, is it somebody I know, is that his Chevy or Allis? Once you are pretty sure, get ready for the wave, which in most cases means letting up the grip on the steering wheel with your right hand, or left if you are left-handed, although many left-handers use the right hand for waves. Be certain to clear a path for your hand or arm: hitting the windshield or part of the vehicle during the wave is considered bad form. Do not lose control of your vehicle. If a wave means driving into a power pole, assume the other person will understand.

WHEN TO WAVE: If you are both in fast vehicles, the waving situation develops and is over before you know it, so wave when the vehicles are about ten yards apart. If you are both in slow vehicles — on tractors say, or driving by the crops real slow in the pickup — the time to wave is pretty important, otherwise the *wave vacuum* can occur: the wave comes too soon, and you are simply passing each other without anything to do. If you wave too soon, it is best to check the pin on the wagon or find out what is under your foot. In fact, many people check equipment up until the time the wave happens, which should be as the vehicles begin passing one another.

Sometimes you come up behind another vehicle, recognize it, and pass it. It is OK, then, to look in the rear-view mirror and wave without looking back, but you should continue looking in the mirror for the return wave from the vehicle behind you. I will say that timing is what distinguishes the professional waver. Getting it down is a matter of practice and maturity. In some ways nothing is sadder than a young person learning to wave and being rebuffed.

KINDS OF WAVES: The right wave is tied in many ways to the waving situation. For fast vehicles, the fingers lifted from the steering wheel will suffice: one to four fingers, never the thumb. If the neighbor has a new pickup and this is the first time you've seen it, then the whole arm and hand is called for, and if it's a four-wheel

4

drive, a couple of toots on the horn would be OK. The tractor to pickup, tractor to combine, wave — when one or both vehicles are slow — commonly involves the hand and the forearm. The upper arm should not move. The elbow gets quite a bit of play here. The simple wave will take care of most situations, but if you just had two inches of rain, a longer wave — with the hand held poised briefly — is perfect. If it rains fourteen inches, make it a small wave and shake your head.

In general, if the situation for the wave is uncommon, as for instance you or the other person have a gutted deer on the hood, then the wave should be a product of the imagination, but usually involves some horizontal as well as vertical movement of the whole arm.

There is no way to deal with everything about waving, and so I leave you with the rule that goes beyond the rules: be yourself as much as possible. If your style is the almost invisible jerk of the arm and hand that leaves your shoulder hurting a little, then by all means wave that way.

If you feel uncomfortable in the country, are not sure how to get into waving, we suggest riding along with a veteran waver, learning as you go.

LEGENDS OF MINNESOTA:
THE DYING RACE

The groves of Minnesota
had a saying
back in the days when
people called Swedes
and Norwegians and Icelanders
started planting trees
to give the eyes a place to rest:
every day one of the leafy children
of the Scandinavians said:
this is a good day for the race.
And another one, not so far away,
would ask: What race?
And the first one would say,
amid the great rolling laughter of trees:
The grove race.

That was a good joke for a hundred years.
Then one day
the descendants of the tree planters
found a new love: it was called land,
open land, and its real name was money.
The horizon was like a king now,
coming back from exile,
and the groves knew they had stood
in his way too long for compromise.
The bulldozers did it
all for hire: they had the hearts
of bank presidents or politicians
who pretend to be dirty
in farming country.
The groves stopped playing around.
They could hardly hear each other
across the distances:
they told stories, said their prayers,
reflected on death,
but had no regrets
and almost no plans for revenge.

LEGENDS OF MINNESOTA:
THE LAST GLACIER

surprised
to feel themselves
warming up
the glaciers of Minnesota
picked their best man
to ride out
the centuries
disguised as a rock

to keep from cracking
in the springs
he thought steadily
of ice
and as much as possible
rested
under his own cool shadow

nobody really knows
what goes through the mind
of a glacier

for one thing he couldn't move
and for another
he was lonely
or maybe the pressure
of being so small
after being so large
did it

anyway

one day
he shouted "GLACIER"
as loud as he could
and exploded
into the Great Blizzard of July
before joining his friends
downstream in the ocean

7

LEGENDS OF MINNESOTA:
THE GARBAGE

One day
the trash in groves
behind farmhouses
began to talk
to itself.

The reason for this
was never found.

People came from the cities
on Sunday
to sit in the bleachers.

After awhile
garbage that talked
became so common
people stopped quoting it.

Then about five years later
a child tossing a can
on top of a garbage pile
was consumed by white fire
and reappeared in three days
bilingual and sun-tanned.

Some people say
the last soup can
completed a figure
described by Christ
in one of the lost parables.
The notion is difficult to prove.

Although it promised nothing
the garbage said
it just wanted to make a movie.
So the garbage made a movie.
And it won an Academy Award
for best special effects
in a short film
by transformed matter.

8

TRAVEL IN MINNESOTA, U.S.A.

Never in all my years in the travel business, have I seen anything like the effect the weakening dollar has had on excursions abroad. Fewer travelers means fewer dollars circulating in the American economy, and quite frankly, fewer dollars coming into the coffers at Ten Thousand Lakes Travel. It was exactly this counter-productive situation that led Ed Mackie, our VP in charge of growth, to an idea that blossomed into increased profits for TTLT and a feather in Minnesota's cap.

What Ed conceptualized was turning the tables on Europe. He said, "Hey, don't we have some sights to see over here?" Of course, he was right, if you will just think for a moment. We began advertising in the foreign newspapers exactly a year ago. The response from the Old World was gratifying, if not enthusiastic. The greenback may be weakening still in major European money markets, but it is strong at home. Enough said. What follows is the promotional literature we presented to our neighbors across the seas.

*   *   *

How long have you dreamed of an American vacation? Wait no longer. Your money will never be worth more than it is now. And what better way to get the flavor of the melting pot of the world than to visit Minnesota, a land-locked state with ten thousand lakes and warm, open people whose homes can be your castles.

All tours to Minnesota include round trip air fare to St. Paul/Minneapolis, the famous "twin" cities, a Minnesota breakfast each day, and lodging. But there are many extras. The details below from our most popular packages are only highlights.

Tour #1, The Midsummer Frolic

Two weeks on a farm in western Minnesota. Accommodations in the upstairs bedroom. A 1962 Chevy straight-stick pickup for your own personal use during the stay (gas and oil extra). If you prefer we can have the truck parked at the airport, with a map taped to the steering wheel. Otherwise, a TTLT representative and the Sky-Blue Girls will welcome you as soon as you touch American soil.

Three hours of American television each night with the host family. Snacks. Escorted trips to the nearest town, where you spend a leisurely afternoon looking in the many shops at the mall. Meet the mayor and his council. Stock car races. Authentic American food of the midwest (lasagna, tacos, chow mein). On Sunday shake the pastor's hand after church. (Or shake the priest's hand. We do ask you to specify if you want the Lutheran Frolic or the Catholic Frolic.) A family reunion at a shelter-house, in season.

Be sure to bring your native costume, as all our guests are given coverage in the local newspaper, complete with a photo of you looking at the front of a bank, surrounded by Minnesota peasants.

Tour #2, The Small-Town Gala

Walk from your lodging (a ranch-style rambler or a bungalow) to the post office to get the mail. Say hello to Americans in their language. Stop off for a large cinnamon roll. The options are nearly infinite. If your cup of tea is immersing yourself in a foreign culture, becoming one of the folks for a few days or weeks, then the Small-Town Gala was designed for you.

Tour #3, The Blizzard Blitz

Very popular with the hardy and adventurous, the Blitz is our one winter excursion. You are guaranteed wind-chill factors of 40 below and loss of electrical power in a small farm home in northern Minnesota. All appropriate clothing is provided, along with a stack of jigsaw puzzles and a cribbage board.

We are adaptable at Ten Thousand Lakes Travel. If the packaged tour is not exactly what you want in American travel, we will do everything possible (and sometimes the impossible) to help you get what you want. Many of our customers have been more than satisfied with the urban experiences we offer. And although we specialize in Minnesota tours, we have, for example, sent a young man from France on a typical family trip to Yellowstone National Park in a recreational vehicle.

If time *and* money are a problem, we still would like to do business with you. *The Economy Fling* includes one big night and two big days with a retired couple of Scandinavian descent. (Gratuities extra.)

Come to Minnesota. Discover for yourself the fabled land of the walleyed pike.

❖   ❖   ❖

The measure of our success at TTLT is probably best illustrated by the fact that some of our "foreign" travelers have lived right here in Minnesota all their lives. But after coming back from one of our tours, they said it was a world they never knew existed, a magical wonderland of delights.

10

CONFESSIONS OF A RURAL BURGLAR

The air's good
but the magic's gone.

Before the doctor
sent me out here for health
we used to joke about the midwest.

It doesn't make any difference
to people that I was the best
second-story man
on the Atlantic coast.
Most of the towns don't even have
second stories.

I started appearing
in daylight
without my disguise
waving back at locals
who recognized me
as the character
from the East.

All the doors are open.
I got sloppy
because nobody cared.
Inside a house
I'd stumble over toys
and the whole family
would wake up to ask
if I was in trouble.
And there I was
at the kitchen table
eating cold roast beef
and sipping cocoa
in the middle of the night.

I knew the price of eggs
and what the almanac said.
If I needed anything
they would help me load it
in the trunk
filling my tank with gas
because they didn't like to think
of me running out
on some lonely road.
I was supposed to come back.

Then I hit country churches
on weekdays
until the echo of small change
made me so nervous
one night I called the sheriff
just to hear an unfriendly voice.

Finally I took
to sitting around a lot
in abandoned farmhouses
getting drunk
on cheap communion wine
living again
old times in Philadelphia.

A MINNESOTA FARMER SPEAKS

I like a good laugh.
Last winter my only milk cow
stood all through the blizzard,
her head to the wind:
when I touched her eyes
they stayed open,
and when I brushed her side
she fell straight over
and hard to the ground.

Now my barn is halfway
to the neighbor's
across fields flattened by hail,
electric wires crossed
in the yard like spaghetti,
the combine and planter
twisted into one machine,
the windmill blade
stuck for good
in the top of my only tree,
the family standing with me
in pajamas at the basement window
listening to other people's troubles
on the battery radio.
I tell them about last April
long after the blizzard
when I found one hog
in his warm cave of snow,
skinny, blind,
barely able to walk:
how he ate out of my hand
even after his strength came back.

It could be worse:
I still have a place to build on
and plenty of lumber to begin.

THE SHORT WAR AGAINST THE SPIRITS
IN MONTEVIDEO, MINNESOTA

Just after Minnesota stopped
being an ocean
for awhile,
just before the glaciers,
and a long time
before the Indians,
spirits began living inside things
like trees:
these were the bodiless monsters
who ate the moon to death.
"Someday," said one spirit
with an unusually loud voice,
"This will be a land
with ten thousand lakes."
Which was a good guess.
They lived in Minnesota
for centuries.
A few intellectuals
broke from the group
over an argument
about whether one could say
"This is true"
and mean it:
although it was a simple semantic
difficulty
semantics had not been invented yet —
nor had the wheel
for that matter.
The skeptics flew to England
inside the bodies
of English sparrows.
Most of them amounted to nothing.

One spirit, for instance,
took up permanent residence
inside stone blocks
because he was sexually frustrated.
Several spirits became kings
or queens, or both.
Another more prolific spirit, though,
actually lived inside the bodies
of Shakespeare, Bacon, Marlowe
and Spenser.
Which explains a lot of things.

Meanwhile the United States
was growing up,
and the spirits from the moon
had already written *Moby Dick*,
Ben Hur, and *Love Story*,
and started the Miss Teenage America
contest, among other things.

However, the bulk of the spirits
decided to settle in Montevideo, Minnesota
for no other reason
than they liked the name,
which means
"I see the mountain"
and is a lie,
there being no mountains
within five hundred miles
of the town.
These spirits sold lumber,
sacked groceries,
drove cars with big tires on the back,
repaired TV sets,
coached football,
and played cards,
mainly Bridge
and Michigan Rummy.

Contrary to public opinion
spirits are normally pretty quiet:
occasionally they might cause their hosts
to fall asleep in church
or make up words like *Montevideans.*
At other times they might congregate
in a fist
and repeatedly strike
a face.
This was known as harmless mischief.

But one day
the spirit who lived inside the man
with an exclusive exercycle franchise
went beserk
after the local radio station
played his favorite country-western song,
"Crazy Arms,"
at the wrong speed.
He began killing cows at night.
The spirit inside the body
of the Sheriff
knew exactly what happened
when he saw the bloodless cow
and no footprints,
but spirits can't tell
on each other.

This happened right around Halloween,
which is when people
dress up in cheap costumes
and pretend to be strange creatures.
Only this time people were really scared:
so they dressed like themselves
on Halloween night
and carried guns.
They were after whatever Thing
killed their cattle
and might next go after
their wives and children.

Nobody was hurt,
but one woman's
weekly production of découpage
was destroyed by gunfire.
The spirits didn't like
any of this.
After an emergency meeting
of the executive committee,
the spirit who went beserk
was sent off for a long rest
and rehabilitation
inside the body of Tammy Wynette.
Then the only problem in Montevideo
was whether
to put up the Christmas decorations
before or after
Thanksgiving.

STAYING WHERE YOU ARE
(A HOME EXERCISE PROGRAM)

In my travels through the States as a Workshop Facilitator, I have run into thousands of super people like myself who were looking for an exercise plan without special equipment, that could be performed in private, and didn't force you to move around unnaturally. This little book is dedicated to them and me. Let's try to do the exercises every day.

TV TUNE. Sit in your reclining lounger, facing the TV set from the usual distance. Begin the exercise by leaning back to the full recline position, keeping your sock feet firmly on the footrest. Count to three before slowly coming to the full up position. Using both hands on the recliner arms, rise, without lunging, until you are standing on both feet. Walk at a normal speed over to the TV set. Stop and bend down, with the right hand extended. Switch channels or adjust the contrast. Straighten up and pivot. Return to the recliner, easing into it with both hands. When you get your wind back, repeat the exercise, alternating left and right hands on the knobs. Do 20 repetitions. Good for the legs, stomach, and eyes.

NATURE WALK. Do this exercise in conjunction with the TV TUNE, if you wish. Instead of returning directly to the recliner, detour by way of the kitchen and bathroom. Keep a steady pace and don't stop for anything in either place. 20 reps. Good for the lower body and will power.

PHONE ANSWER. Lying on the couch, pretend that the phone rings, or make your own ringing noise. Hop up to get it. Changing hands with each rep, bring the receiver quickly to your ear and the mouthpiece to your mouth. Say hello. Nod your head several times. Say goodbye and return to the couch. Lie down and close your eyes for a count of five. 10 reps. Good for the neck, forearms, ears, and mouth.

TABLE SCOOT. Sit on a chair in front of the kitchen table. Gripping each side of the seat with your hands, bend rapidly forward while pulling the chair. You should end up with your stomach about five inches from the table edge. Put your elbows on the table. Bring one hand, then the other, to your face, just below the nose. Grip the seat again, thrusting backwards to your original position. 15 reps. Good for the Achilles tendon, thighs, buttocks, and elbows.

PAPER BEND. This exercise can be done in bare feet or slippers. Beginning in the kitchen or bedroom, walk briskly to the front door. Rotate the knob with alternate hands on each rep. Open the door and bend forward at the waist, so that your head and upper body are sticking out at a forty-five degree angle. Look to the left and right for the newspaper. Return to your starting point. 15 reps. Good for the legs, back, neck, and fingers.

LOST AND FOUND. You can do this one wherever you have room to crawl. Pretend that you have dropped something that is small and round and it has disappeared. Get down on your hands and knees, after an initial walk around the room. Crawl back and forth in a random pattern, bending your head to the floor and peering under the couch, stove, or refrigerator when you pass. Do this for two minutes. Good for the arms, legs, knees, and toes.

SOCK PULL. Assume a standing position in your bare feet. Take a sock in two hands, slightly stretching the opening. As you lower your arms, bring one foot up and put the sock on. Repeat with the other foot. Remove the socks. 5 reps. This exercise uses all the muscles in the arms and legs, especially if you dance around on your foot. If you fall down, get right back up.

CIGARETTE LIGHT. Shake a cigarette from a soft pack. Alternate left and right hands. Bring the cigarette toward your face as you bend your head down. Put it between your lips. Bring the other hand to the end of the cigarette and click the lighter with your thumb. Keep the elbows fairly high. Hold the cigarette in your mouth for a count of five. Return it to the pack. 30 reps. You may light the cigarette and inhale at the end of the exercise. Good for the triceps, neck, and lips.

HITTING THE SACK. Stand by the bed in your bare feet and pajamas. Pull the covers back. Then, in a series of movements hard to describe, jump into bed and slide under the covers, pulling them swiftly to the chin. Reach behind your head with both hands and position the pillow. Flip onto one side and then the other, exhaling loudly. While on your side, lift your head and punch the pillow with the free hand. Flop around briefly, until you are face down. Return to your back in one motion. Raise your feet, pulling the covers high into the air for a count of two. Lower them. Push the covers off now and sit up on the edge of the bed, with your head between your hands and your elbows on your knees. Count to five and stand up straight. Make the bed. 5 reps. Good for every part of the body.

Those of you who like to get fresh air from time to time might be interested in my second little book, *Moving Outdoors*. The same philosophy is at the heart of these exercises, which include CARRYING THE GARBAGE CAN, RAISING THE GARAGE DOOR, STARTING THE MOWER, CHANGING THE STORMS, and LOOKING UNDER THE HOOD TO SEE WHAT THAT KNOCKING SOUND IS.

EXPLANATIONS ATTACHED

The self-sticking label does not describe
the place I have always lived.
No number listed matches my occupation.
Even when my wife and I file separately
we are doing it jointly.
I see no provision for combining ourselves
exactly as we want to.
We depend on each other.

Yes, we definitely wish to itemize
the following deductions from last year:

1. Our income was not as gross
as it could have been.
For this we are thankful.

2. We have an annuity sheltered from taxes,
our daughter, new to you.
We expect life-long dividends.

3. Our garden created phenomenal returns
on an investment of nearly nothing.
It was our main source of interest.

Signed on the bottom line, I declare
that everything I have said is true.

PATTERNS IN WINTER

The blizzard builds one drift
outside the chicken shed
five feet high and shaped
exactly like a chicken hawk
looking in through the broken window.
Snowmobiles make one track
over the smooth white of ditches:
their noise breaks open the air
of a cold morning,
they are always going someplace
fast, and when two go by,
the drivers' voices carry for miles.
And all over Minnesota in parking lots,
cars are nose to nose, two slim wires
holding them together,
one head under the hood steaming,
the other cranking with a key,
his chin resting on the steering wheel,
leaning in the direction he wants to go:
when it starts, a winter joy, and hands
waving thank you, Merry Christmas,
Bon Voyage: the hoods slam shut,
the snow tires squeak toward the road
that connects the car to the garage.
The next season is spring.

DEAR SERIOUS WRITER

Thank you for your submission to *Serious Times*. Many of the stories, poems, and articles we receive are simply not serious. Writers must not take us at our word, or else feel that writing something amusing or cute will be an antidote to living in serious times. Whatever the reason, we reject all humorous writings without comment. Your submission, however, is not funny, and we commend you on that. It is quite a talent to be able to make people serious, through serious writing. Still, we cannot accept your offering, because it is not serious enough, according to two of our editors, well-known serious writers who have been making people serious for years.

You don't make anybody laugh here, or even smile, but in paragraph three there is a lightness surfacing. You set the tone quite well in the opening, with that quick somberness approaching melancholy, the *sine qua non* of serious writing. Paragraph two keeps up the pace until the last sentence, when the reversal of clauses and the overuse of modifiers gives a buoyancy to your prose, to your subject, and subsequently to your reader. If you had bounced back in paragraph three with something very serious in the first sentence, I think the slow spot at the end of paragraph two would have been overlooked. But you do not. Paragraph three keeps rising, and paragraph four stays at that level. After that you do return to the slow and serious pace of the opening. In fact, your conclusion is masterful, showing us that you have the wherewithal to make it as a serious writer. That is why we have taken time with your manuscript. Funny writers, those who send us the witty tales, the gags, the satirical fantasies, are everywhere: it is the serious writer who is scarce. If we find one with potential, like yourself, we encourage him or her. Congratulations. You have that rare talent for making people serious. We hope to hear more from you.

SCHOOL CLOSINGS

Okay, we're gonna run through those school closings, delays, and postponements one more time for our listening audience.

No school, no school, no school at all today in the following schools. Now this is all we have for now. No school, no school today in Agwater, public and parochial, no morning kindergarten. Let's say if we don't say so, then there will be no parochial, no public, and no kindergarten in the rest of the school closings. Okay. School closings for today, from the beginning. No school in Agwater, Chikhill, Fildhole-Beerington, Grand Goose. Now that's public only. Parochial will be in session in Grand Goose today, but don't bring your workbooks or the felt animals. Okay. Now we're back to total closings, everything shut down in the following towns, school-wise. Jerome-Julian, Burly, Pitnose, Choo-Choo, Carrigan-Roby, Bog, Woody, Winton, Going, Hello, Five Corners, Treeville, Lake Village, Pleasant Hill. Okay. Pleasant Hill is having, we repeat, is having *afternoon* kindergarten. Evidently, according to the principal, all the afternoon kids live in town and can get together at Miss Galeburn's apartment at the normal time. Okay. That's about it on the school closings.

Now, these are the delays, school and buses two hours late, unless we say different, in Calley, Winon, Wabasha, Barton, Lavage, Flintstone, Urania. Okay now. In Urania school for the town kids will start at 9:15 instead of 8:30, and those riding buses will follow this schedule. Bus number four will not stop at the Raymond Mark place, because Mr. Graham thinks he wouldn't be able to get her started again, not on that hill. Bus number three will not run. It has not been running for a couple of days now, they think it's the carburetor. Bus number one and bus number two will be two hours late as usual. That's in Urania.

Okay now. We're back to straight two hours late for schools and buses, public and parochial. Turner, Standoff, WaWa, Cordelia. Okay. In Cordelia bus number two will not go out. Superintendent Bond said that the driver said something about they didn't pay him enough to drive out in the middle of a blizzard. Otherwise, school and buses two hours late in Cordelia. Kane, Kopley, Hilmar. Okay now. In Hilmar only the basketball team will be picked up. Well, you can understand that. They're unbeaten in fifteen starts and have a good chance for the State title. Okay, now, good luck to you Hilmar Harriers. Norwich, Nyung, Border, Rufton. School and buses two hours late. Okay. We'll repeat those closings and delays in a few minutes. We kind of expect some of the late starts to close down. It doesn't look so bad right here in town, but out in the country evidently there's quite a wind. So if you don't have someplace real important to go, we advise you to stay where you are.

Okay now. On the postponements. No afternoon bowling in the Forty But Not Fat league today. No Rocky Mountain oyster supper at Jig's Farm and Home. That will be held next Tuesday, all you can eat, with the trimmings. Okay now. Let me read this announcement from the Highway Patrol. As of right now the local office of the Highway Patrol is advising no travel at all, none, in the area. Some roads are impassable and others are drifting fast. So okay, stay off those roads and stay tuned here.

Okay now. The bank robbery scheduled for noon today at the Savings and Loan will be postponed indefinitely. That's gotta be a joke. Okay. The Jaycee-ettes will not practice today. Learn your parts though. Okay. Crazy Days is cancelled until next Tuesday. All those bargains will be available again on Tuesday, for CRAZEEE DAZE, and boy, let me tell you, they were going raving mad, just nuts, down there at Bob's Bootery. And at B and B Clothing they were dropping everything but their pants, Garwin said. But that's all off till next Tuesday. The Chamber of Commerce says the merchants can keep the clown suits and big noses till next week.

After these emergency announcements, we'll get back to school closings. Will the driver of the red Volkswagen, license number AZ 234, please call his mother. And Elmer Vishy is supposed to get back home, but if he goes by a store be sure to pick up some two percent, they're out.

24

OLD FAITHFUL

The title stands frozen
waiting for the poem.
This is snapshot verse.
There is the geyser
smoking into the air.
Notice the bird flying
through the steam.
Near me tourists have risen
to applaud: I feel let down.
My daughter loves it
but wonders where the bears are.
Afterwards we pass the electronic sign
announcing the next burst,
people already replacing us
on the benches.
We eat cold potatoes and gravy
in the Yellowstone cafeteria,
we walk once through the Yellowstone drugstore,
we climb into the car at dusk
and leave by the east exit,
all alone, three of us,
in the dark: nobody is coming in
at this hour. What we remember
is the amazing closeness of the road,
the tightness of the park,
the relief of getting out,
getting on down the highway
to Cody, Wyoming: another place
we keep our camera in the trunk for.

WINTER MOON

At 3:31 a.m. CST I see the moon
out the kitchen window looking like earth.
The wind is dead. The snow has stopped.
I check the thermometer. **Zero.**
In my storm coat and knee-high boots
I step into the moon of snow
moving like an astronaut
demonstrating gravity to children.
I run down a hill, leaping high,
powder snow sticking to my legs.
My footprints have clean edges.
I feel like the beginning of a church.
After one somersault I go back.
My impressions last till morning.

THE OWL

The wail of the owl
half wakes my daughter
from the deep sleep
of a day at kindergarten:
the sympathetic moans
make me think of losing her.

We live on a world
made familiar
by long acquaintance,
but there is nothing stranger
than the wind, and the sun,
and rain, and lightning:
or the owl's cry
and the groans of an only child,
or the stillness
of a September night,
or the people you won't see
again before they do
what is known on earth
as die.

THE WIDOW BEFORE THE AUCTION

Spread out on the lawn,
lined up in front of the barn,
it looks like so little
but it's most everything we owned:
it all goes, all of it.
Dying's hard enough
without watching the machinery
rust. And the quilts,
I can't stand the empty places
underneath them on the bed.
The photos I kept,
but there's not one picture
of him working.
I don't know how it happened:
that's how I remember him,
heading out to the fields
on top of the John Deere,
scooping grain, walking
among the cattle: right now
I can smell his clothes,
the way they were on the porch
when he came in for dinner.
Well, all the rest goes,
like him
on the usual terms.
Seeing it out the window
will be the worst:
so many strangers
shoulder to shoulder
having a good time.
I wish he'd be there,
bidding. I wonder what he'd buy.
Anyway I'd just like to watch him
even if his back was to me.
I loved the way he moved:
his body was always a wonder to me,
and familiar as my own.

THE GESTURE

It is the hottest day of summer
and it hasn't rained for a week.
We are going through the beans
with the shields off. The water
in the thermos tastes like dust.
An old neighbor died three days ago.
He could still find wheel ruts
that were part of the trail to Fargo once.
In front of me the hired man
sees the funeral getting out
at the Swan Lake Church:
all the coats and ties are gone.
The cars pull onto the road
to take the body to the burial ground
in town. When the hearse goes by
the hired man stops his tractor
and raises the cultivator.
He does not start again
until the last car disappears
in a watery mirage on the tar.
I do the same: but it's not
repetition that makes manners bad,
it's not knowing what to do
the first time something happens.

OLD UPRIGHT IN GOOD CONDITION

After years of not practicing
Al was looking for a piano.
What he had in mind
was a baby grand
with one ivory gone
and a history that went back
to the RAF pilot who played Haydn
before every mission out of Brisbane.
But we answered the ad anyway.
The four of us drove together
twenty miles south in the rain
as the sun went down in gray.
Every turn onto narrower roads
made us consider the strength
of fairy tales.

The old couple met us
at the farmhouse door,
and took us across the kitchen,
uphill, to the dark place
called the parlor.
The piano was nearly upright
and covered by photographs
of all their children
in different stages of growing up.
The piano had not been used
since it was bought for the son
who hated lessons, they told us,
and later went into the roofing business.

Al couldn't make it play a tune
any of us could recognize,
the top would not open,
and half the keys were stuck down
like the pedals.

We stayed for their whole story
but we didn't want the piano.
It would have sucked up music for miles
and ground it into dust,
it would have brought on the ice ages,
glad of the frozen songs:
and it would have taken a glacier
to move it out from under the children
in the solid granite parlor.

Yeah, I know where that is, but let me think what's the best way to get there. You go . . . you go . . . no, that's not it. That used to be a shortcut but it's filled in there in one spot, so that's out. Now, where did you say you're from, over by Cloister? So you came in on twelve there, just east of the grain elevator. That makes it a little easier, because if you come in on five that road looks like it runs straight with the compass but it don't. It sits squeehunky. People in town have got used to it, but they don't like it. It throws you off every time. Where it turns into Prairie Street, a couple of people put corner windows in their houses so they could look one true direction in the morning. Anyway, that's neither here nor there.

Let's see, one way you can go is to take a left at the Reformed Church, but that's not the best way. I'd say go on down this street, the way you're pointed, until you come to the wide place by the trailer court. The road you want turns right. You can't miss it. There's a big sign that says STATE BASEBALL REGIONAL RUNNERUPS IN 1954. You could go straight there, but I wouldn't. If you go left you'll soon know, because that road just ends with no warning, up against a mountain of sand the County put there for something. So you've turned right. You want to keep going, past the welding shop, past the Used-A-Little, out past the Golden Manor Haven, say about three miles. You turn left, or not turn left really, just sort of slant off. If you go straight on there you come to the landfill, but it's closed now. So you're going down that slanty left road. You'll know it's the right one because in about three quarters of a mile there's a broken culvert on one side of the road and a set of rusty wheel weights for a John Deere leaning against the power pole on the other side. Don't ask me why they don't pick those things up.

It gets a little tricky here, but it's the best way. You've passed the wheel weights and you're going east. You go four, maybe five, miles until you hit the dip where the road washed out in '75. Right after that there's a bridge with most of the railing gone on the left side. Mort Andersen left the wings down going home with the eight-row cultivator. Anyway you can't miss it.

The first thing you see after the bridge is a scrubby bunch of boxelder trees. Some people say there's no other kind. Take a right. There used to be a big pile of steel fence posts on the corner but somebody hauled them off. You go a few miles, three, maybe four, around the lake, until you pass the duck boat with the bottom gone.

32

By the way, that's a good walleye lake, but nobody got too many last year. The weather's been funny. It didn't hurt the bullheads though. After the boat you come to an intersection. Don't be looking for a freeway or anything. You've been on a dirt road since you turned off the gravel at the boxelders. Now I'd say just stop and sit for a minute. You'll see corn ahead of you, oat stubble on the left, alfalfa on the right, and of course in the rearview mirror you'll see the lake.

Go left there and just follow the curve of the road. Turn right at the upside-down combine, right again at the burnt-out farmhouse with the overalls flying from the windmill. When you come to the two junk cars in the ditch, you should be able to see where you're going with no problem. As I say, this is the best way. There is another way, but you would have to go north. This way you can't miss it.

Please read this entire letter carefully MR. H. MOHR OF COT-TONWOOD, for within the next few minutes you will be asked to make a decision that could change your whole life there in LYON COUNTY MINNESOTA, MR. MOHR. We want you to subscribe to *The Magazine* and have it delivered to your home at RURAL ROUTE COTTONWOOD. Imagine the envy of your neighbors, THE BUYSSES AND THE BJORNSONS.

You don't have to subscribe to *The Magazine*, MR. H. MOHR OF COTTONWOOD, but if you don't, you and your lovely wife, MRS. J. MOHR OF COTTONWOOD, could be surprised on November 12 at precisely 4 a.m. by a man in a dark suit, MR. STUBEN OF DETROIT, who will politely ask you to subscribe, once. We think you will like *The Magazine*, but if you don't like it, lump it, MR. AND MRS. H. MOHR OF COTTONWOOD. The longer you wait to reply, the greater the chance our computer, MR. FORTRAN OF NEW HAVEN, could mistakenly dispatch from the MINNE-APOLIS AIRPORT a speaker truck that would drive down the STREETS OF COTTONWOOD broadcasting unpleasant rumors about you and EVERYONE IN THE MOHR FAMILY. For each day you delay, the chance increases that your family, MR. H. MOHR OF COTTONWOOD, would be seen driving through LYON COUNTY MINNESOTA in a brand-new luxury car on its way to an undisclosed place.

We are sure you will like our magazine and will want a lifetime subscription. MR. BJORNSON likes our magazine. Ask him. The lovely family of MR. JACK PETERSON, JUST SOUTH OF YOU IN LYON COUNTY, did not like our magazine. You, MR. H. MOHR OF COTTONWOOD, bought one of their coffee tables at the estate auction.

In any case, just put the computer card in the envelope marked *Yes* or in the envelope marked *No*. But if you insert the computer card in the envelope marked *No*, we suggest you dress yourself, MR. H. MOHR OF COTTONWOOD, in a flak suit.
Sincerely,
The Magazine

AFTER THE STORM

Get out
your
golf balls
tennis balls
baseballs
softballs
racquet balls
squash balls
volley balls
soccer balls
basket balls
beach balls
if it is not
one of these sizes
it is not hail.

RALPH NADER VISITS MY HOUSE

Coming home late one night I find him
under the kitchen sink with a flashlight
taking down the names of canned goods.
I know it's him.
He shines the light in my face.
He reads from his list:
"Artificial colors, bulging tops,
barbituates and chemical garbage.
And this is only a beginning.
Sit down please."
I sit down, shielding my eyes,
trying to make out his face.
"Crawling between your walls
I discovered mice nested among wires.
The water heater has no safety valve.
Your attic is ticking."
"But . . . " I say.
He smiles. "The fully documented account
of the accidents you will have
is to be published in Friday's *New York Times*."
The chair collapses when I stand,
light bulbs pop out of their sockets,
my shoe laces burst into flames.
"Your wife is also defective," he sneers,
climbing out the window
avoiding my dangerous doors.

ESCAPE ARTIST

you hear about me daily
before the chuckle
at the end of the news

shot fourteen times
by a wounded husband
who thought I was somebody
else, I am released
from the hospital
before the smoke clears
both lungs and my heart
resting safely on the right

buried all during
the Christmas holidays
in an old well
I am found playing cards
upside down, winning

I have drunk twelve full
ounces of formaldehyde
in a Coke bottle
and walked away
the going easy

taking the ditch
to avoid oncoming cars
with broken parts
I flip end over end
and land on all four tires
my foot in the carburetor:
I race along the ditch
hit the small rise
at the edge of the river
leap the water
and claw with power
up the opposite bank:
I spin into a field of corn
trailing barbed wire
until I see the road again:
I drive home
in a total loss
honking waving smiling

I lighten people's day

MY LIFE, THE MOVIE

I'll admit I'm only up to where I get my first guitar, but when I finish I know who I want to play me in the movie, if you do use my book to make a movie. I'm putting in the good and the bad, so it won't just be a rosy picture. We all have our hard knocks. I think Al Pacino. He's one hell of an actor and a fine guy. I have always admired him. Now my first girlfriend, Sally, I loved her but never told her and always regretted it. The guy she married was a loser. Him you can run over with a diesel, if you don't mind. Sally should be played by Tatum O'Neal or Sissy Spacek. That's what she was like, you know, sexy and young and a knockout. Later, when I'm a success, could you have me meet up with her? I think it might happen someday anyway and probably will make a better movie. It sure would make me happier. My wife says she sees herself as Jane Fonda. I don't know where she's looking, but go ahead.

My folks said all the movie stars they know are dead, so they'll leave it up to you. They raised me in a log cabin in west Texas, but they've left there and have a pretty nice place in Ft. Lauderdale. They told me that a lot of their friends don't know about the dump they used to live in, so if you could, let me be born in a ranch house. Humble but nice. And if it's not too much trouble, could you put an oil well in the back yard, even if it's only fifty barrels a day?

My younger sister (Diane Keaton) says don't show her before she lost her baby fat and got over the complexion problem. My idea would be to have her live with her aunt (Barbra Streisand) and just write letters. My older sister says she doesn't care if she's in or not, and as far as she's concerned she can be played by R2-D2. I say leave her out, with that attitude. One sister and a brother is enough anyway. E.J. figures Burt Reynolds would be OK for him. One thing though, could you give E.J. a custom '55 Chevy when he graduates from high school? The folks only had enough for the first payment on a four-door Dodge with burnt valves and E.J. has always felt bad about that, and the folks too.

The wife says if you could, please put in another bathroom and change the drapes in the living room. She would just be humiliated if anybody saw the rags she has up there now. Also, we don't have any kids, but we wouldn't mind a good breed of dog that could do tricks.

Things haven't been going so good lately with my career, but I expect it's just a natural slump, so when you get to this part, just go ahead and put me on a big city tour. Make it one to celebrate my first gold album, with a song on it called "Down But Not Out, Clawing To Get Up." You should have me run into Sally about here, maybe when we do Austin. And I need some new clothes.

The main thing is to get my life right, to show how I had lots of help from everybody and thank the Lord for every success and am proud to have humble roots. Just tell it like it is, in technicolor.

Laying Back this month has again published many books of interest to readers like you who have chosen an alternative life. A finer set of books we have not seen in a long time. They are available from us at natural prices.

Living Off the Land, by Eliot and Grisly Pirot, presents a unique system based on the notion that living *on* the land is unhealthy because of the dirt, insects, and the possibility of direct contact with germs inherent to soil. This book outlines, with joy and feeling, the Pirot's experiment with living one year six and a half inches above the ground in a structure made entirely of styrofoam packing from stereo and TV crates.

Building Your Own Fly Swatter, by "Pete," is another in the series of self-help books designed for the beginner and intermediate. Interspersed with quotations from Lorca, Rilke, Hesse, Colette, and people "Pete" met on the road, the book is readable even if you do not want to build your own fly swatter. But if you do, here is the book: there is nothing else to be said about the theory and practice of this amazing tool. *Building Your Own Fly Swatter* is "Pete's" first book since *Old Wire*.

Minimal Farming, by Gale Breeze, is for those who do not have their own "place." Gale, a retired account executive who sold everything except his blue chips in order to lay back, filled his modest three-room house in the city with loam and began farming under fluorescent lights in his bedroom, bathroom, and living room. The best chapter in this inspiring book is "Year-round Kohlrabi." Highly recommended.

Natural Musical Instruments, by A. T. Bister, is most refreshing. Tired of AM radio, hi-fi, live concerts, and the plethora of ordinary instruments that are over-priced by the music establishment, Mr. Bister remembered his father's ability to play simple tunes on the hood of his pickup. Here are plans for simple instruments made from such things as rhubarb leaves, tomato juice cans, tube-type tires, and rocks. Mr. Bister tells how he tuned his house one windy day by adjustment of the windows and ended up with an instrument that could play classic blues. We were especially thrilled with his description of the toilet bowl bass and the rusty nail dulcimer.

Ultimate Compost, by Bob Bozley, is a remarkable book. A combination of a natural dieting book for those living too long on the fat of the land, a religious system, and a composting manual, this attractively illustrated volume explains in detail how everything organic is turned into manure. Beef, nitrite-ridden bacon, head lettuce, waxed delicious apples, in fact all supermarket food, is simply brought home, but not inside, unwrapped, and placed in the composter, where it provides, in a matter of weeks, a good fertilizer for the garden. When the garden comes in, it also is composted. Starting with a one acre country site, Bozley, a thin, monk-like former baseball umpire, was able to put himself in touch with the universe and now knows who his friends are. After three years he owns twelve acres of rich compost north of Duluth, Minnesota.

Odd Sources of Energy, by Olag Pothansen, outlines how Olag powers his house with traffic noise on the freeway near his home during the day, and at night harnesses the darkness. The whole system was built with stuff Olag bought at garage sales. An exciting book, not for the dabbler.

Also recommended: *Burning Your Logs at Both Ends, Cross-Country Skiing in Summer, Environmental Pollution in Eden, Raising Children Organically,* and *The Hand-carved Typewriter.*

TO MY FRIEND WHO IS NOT SAFETY CONSCIOUS AND SOMETIMES ARCHLY

It comes to me
in times exactly like this one:
I am driving at night,
steady as a religious fanatic
five miles below the limit.
I dim my lights with precision.

And there you are
in a black coat
walking your brown dog
on the center line,
reflecting nothing
I can see
until too late.

I must choose between you
and your dog.
I think how unhappy your wife will be
with either choice.

I do not touch the brakes,
I do not swerve.
I stay in my lane.
I let the law decide.

LUCAS TOWNSHIP

In Lucas Township
after the blizzard
a frozen dog
cantilevered into space
near our border:
this was clearly not
one of ours.
All our dogs
know better.

Driving County 22
the air changes
at the invisible line
between Lucas
and the other places:
people pronounce Hello
with strange accents,
the finger wave
from the steering wheel
lacks sincerity:
those people want our
land, our wives,
they want to make us
like them.

In Lucas we mainly drive
Chevys
and those who don't
have good reasons.
We believe in God
and have our own
interpretation of the Bible.

We are forming a University
for our children.

But don't think we want
you here:
we can recognize a stranger
long before
he crosses the border,
practicing yesterday's
password.

AT EVERY GAS STATION THERE ARE MECHANICS
WHO HEAR MY POEMS
for Steve Dunn

When I get my car fixed
I know what is wrong:
I describe the malfunction
like one whose only interest
in life is driving
down a road with no trouble
under the hood.
I get results.

Later I mention my poems
and the mechanic's hand
drops the box-end wrench
on his foot:
he looks beyond the grease rack
and rows of shock absorbers.
He would clearly give anything
to be checking compression,
but I recite a poem anyway.
He likes it,
but doesn't know what it's for
or how it works.
His one nightmare, he says,
is a clean sheet of paper
that's supposed to have something on it.
My car takes me home to the typewriter.

BEING POSITIVE

Because I grew up in a family where distrust and sarcasm were a way of life, I developed a negative outlook. I know that being negative is not very positive, so I'm working on it. I don't mean to imply that I've been reborn or something. I'm just trying to be more positive. You can't imagine how hard it is. On Thanksgiving our family used to get up late and watch parades on TV so we could hurl cutting remarks at the floats and bands, for each other's benefit. After a while somebody was elected to walk three blocks to McDonald's for the big bag of burgers and fries. Christmas, of course, was a grim, dark, and oppressive day. Our only tradition was to stand around K-Mart on Christmas Eve and laugh at the Blue-Light Specials: sock sets for Dad, motorized manger scenes, Gomer Pyle's sacred album.

But as I said, I'm trying to put that behind me. It's a job, though. We expected strangers to be crooked, especially if there was an exchange of money. They all wanted to gyp you, they were out to get you, to do you in: they had something up their sleeve, they were part of a fly-by-night outfit. Our family knew that nobody ever does anything for nothing. Door-to-door salesmen were the enemy. A couple of people down the block had signs on their doors that said NO PEDDLERS. Our sign just said, IF YOU CAN READ THIS YOU ARE STANDING ON THE SPOT WHERE TWO SALESMEN WERE SHOT AND KILLED. It scared off Girl Scouts and Brownies, too, but that wasn't our idea, because some of those kids wouldn't think of stealing the cookie money or putting dog turds in the peanut clusters.

Even if you're a person who always looks on the sunny side, you can sympathize, I'm sure. If you build a relationship on mutual trust, somebody can take advantage of you before you know it. That makes sense, you see, but you don't have to overdo it. That's what I'm trying to correct. I'm trusting people more and looking for the silver lining. I'll tell you one thing, though: I didn't go to a therapist to find out how to improve my attitude. If you can't depend on yourself, who can you depend on? I woke up one morning and said to myself that I would try to be cheery, compassionate, and positive. It would never have occured to me to see a therapist. First of all, there's nothing really wrong with being negative. It's not a disease. Anyway, a therapist mainly makes money doing what people could do for themselves. If you want to be more positive, do it. Don't spend fifty dollars a week talking to some guy with a soft monotone.

I don't have a system or a plan to follow. It's slow going, but what else is new? Miracles rarely happen, and if they do they don't happen overnight. Besides, if you start looking for revelation, the flash of light and angels singing on high, you're getting into the area of religion. Before you know it you're in over your head.

I started at home. If I had started being more positive at work, they would have suspected something. Now when I come out of the bedroom in the morning, I greet the family with a fairly positive *Hello*. I'm aware that most people say *Good Morning*, but I'm only trying to be positive not a messiah. I used to say either nothing or *What's Wrong?* I still say that, but only if something is wrong when I get up, which is about twice a week. But that's not bad. I have a good breakfast. That doesn't mean granola and yoghurt: some people can stomach that stuff, but I can't. I'm talking about bacon and eggs, with coffee. You put that in front of me and I feel positive till noon, unless something goes haywire at work.

I don't even know why I'm telling you all this. Before I began changing my outlook I would have made a face and said something sharply ironic about now. I guess I'm trying to share with you my ideas on being positive. I'm not trying to share my whole life, or get into intimate details, spilling my guts. That would be a ridiculous spectacle. But I did want to tell you, I suppose. If you don't want to listen, that's all right, don't feel obligated. I'll live.

Let me give you some examples of how to be more positive. Don't take these literally. They're just models. Say you go to a movie with a bunch of people and afterwards the usual discussion takes place. Well, before this I would have said, "I drove ten miles in heavy traffic to watch two people talk about divorce in a dark apartment?" Now I would say, "That movie wasn't very depressing." You can see the improvement. Say somebody you know buys a new car and, of course, drives over for you to see it. Obviously you're supposed to make a positive remark after you've looked at the dual ignition system, the instrument cluster, and the sun roof. This happened last week, so I said, "A lot of people don't ever have trouble with these cars." I won't tell you what kind it was. You have to live and learn.

Maybe you want to insulate your house, if you're lucky enough to own one and can afford insulation after the property taxes. You decide on the foam insulation, the stuff that goes in gooey and gets hard inside the walls. Think of it this way: You want a warmer house (positive). You are hiring a person who needs work (positive). Your house will have a higher resale value (positive). You are helping to reduce fuel consumption (positive). See? Now if the insulation is put in under high pressure and squeezes into the window cavities and makes bulges in the walls, very calmly and cheerfully try to get your money back before you sue the company. If that doesn't work, just ask around until you find somebody else who got taken to the cleaners, and see if their house is filled with formaldehyde fumes, too. Communicate with them, talk it over, share with them. See?

As I said, I'm not trying to save the world. I'm only trying to be more positive. Maybe you don't even care. It wouldn't surprise me. If I stuck my neck out here and failed, what's the big deal? You can't win 'em all. In fact you're lucky to win one or two. You've got to roll with the punches. Keeping your guard up doesn't hurt either.

DEATH BY CAR

> "The most popular time for dying
> on American highways is one o'clock
> Sunday morning." — public service announcement

If I die
on an American highway
let it be a single car accident
on Tuesday afternoon
at three o'clock.
Let my car be undamaged,
upright on the shoulder,
the engine idling smoothly,
the gearshift at neutral,
the radio on to weather.
Let me be dead behind the wheel,
foot on the brake,
looking ahead
through the clear windshield.
Let me be the local man
who dies of undetermined injuries
at an unpopular time
on a cloudless day.
Let me be under investigation
for weeks.
Let there be mysterious circumstances.

Mash together pterodactyls, enormous ferns, and other living things whose time has come. Press well under tons of dirt and rock for a few million years at high heat, till done. This will create a black gooey substance thousands of feet below the surface of the earth. While the organic matter is cooking, discover the wheel. Domesticate horses. Make a cart. *Hook the horses to the front of the cart.* Ride that way for a while. See how you like it. Put some springs on the cart if the ride is too firm. Enclose the seat to protect yourself from the elements. Ride around some more, nodding at your neighbors. Put a little fringe on it. The black gooey substance should be about ready now. See if it burns. If it does, invent the steam engine. Don't rush things. Rest awhile. Then invent the internal combustion engine. Think hard. *Take the internal combustion engine and mount it on the cart.* Leave all the other stuff on the cart, including the wheels. Shoot the horses. Drive around in your horseless cart until you feel the need for rubber tires, fenders, self-starters, windshields. Try that for awhile. Then decide to get where you're going faster. Put a bigger engine on your cart. Streamline the frame. Eventually add a spoiler, a hood scoop, and a tape deck. Use an on-board computer for determining miles per gallon, distance to destination, estimated time of arrival. Drive around like this for a while, listening to Barry Manilow. Make sure your insurance is paid up. Put a sticker on your bumper. "Enjoy the Ride," it says: "Nothing Lasts Forever."